ANIMALS
ANIMALS

CAMELS

BY JUDITH JANGO-COHEN

BENCHMARK BOOKS

MARSHALL CAVENDISH

Series Consultant
James Doherty
General Curator
Bronx Zoo, New York

To Molly Morrison, editor, with thanks.
–j.j.c.

Benchmark Books
Marshall Cavendish
99 White Plains Road
Tarrytown, NY 10591–9001
www.marshallcavendish.com

Library of Congress Cataloging-in-Publication Data

Jango-Cohen, Judith.
Camels / Judith Jango-Cohen.
p. cm. – (Animals, animals)
Includes bibliographical references (p.) and index.
Contents: Introducing camels – A camel's diet – Blasting sand and blazing sun – Birth and growth – From caravan to race track.
ISBN 0-7614-1750-8
1. Camels–Juvenile literature. [1. Camels.] I. Title. II. Series.

QL737.U54J36 2004
599.63'62–dc22
2003024842

Photo Research by Joan Meisel
Front cover: Frans Lemmens/Getty Images

Photographs in this book are used by permission and through the courtesy of: *Corbis*: Bernard & Catherine Desjeux, 12; Liba Taylor, 14; Keren
Su, 16; Owen Franken, 18; Dave G. Houser, 31; Philip Marazzi/Papilio, 34. *Getty Images*: Joseph J. Scherschel, 4; Chris Dyball/Innerlight, 10; Frans
Lemmens, 20-21; Penny Tweedie, 25; Art Wolfe, 32-33. *Peter Arnold*: Henry Ausloos, 22; Tompix, 26; Fred Bruemmer, 28; Jeffrey Rottman, 36;
Milan Horacek/Bilderberg, 39; Hans-Jürgen Burkard/Bilderberg, 40-41; Still Pictures, 42.

Printed in China
1 3 5 6 4 2

CONTENTS

1

INTRODUCING CAMELS

Two scientists crouch behind a scrawny shrub and peer out from between the branches. Up ahead, three Bactrian camels emerge from the dunes. Each camel has a thick coat and two hairy humps that look like haystacks. As the camels ramble closer, one scientist clicks a picture. The lead camel freezes, staring at the intruders. The camels race away, spraying sand.

Wild Bactrian camels are rare, skittish, and difficult to study. Scientists believe there are only 1,500 to 3,000 of them left in the world. They wander the mountainous regions of southwest Mongolia and northwest China. In these dry grasslands and deserts, freshwater is scarce, so wild Bactrians survive by drinking from salty springs.

Most of the world's Bactrian camels do not live in wild herds. They are *domestic* animals, tamed and raised by people. Domesticated Bactrians live in China and Mongolia like their wild relatives, and in areas as far west as Turkey.

WHITE CAMELS ARE PRIZED FOR THEIR SOFT, FLUFFY COATS.

There is another *species*, or kind, of camel besides the two-humped Bactrian. This is the one-humped Arabian. Arabians have longer legs and slimmer bodies than the Bactrians. They also have a shorter coat because they live in warmer regions. Arabian camels are widespread in Arabia, the Sahara desert, and Australia. They also live in Iran, Afghanistan, and Turkey, with the Bactrian.

BACTRIAN CAMELS WEIGH ABOUT 1,400 POUNDS (635 KG) AND ARE ABOUT 7.5 FEET (229 CM) TALL AT THE SHOULDER.

ARABIAN CAMELS WEIGH ABOUT 1,100 POUNDS (500 KG) AND ARE ABOUT 7 FEET (213 CM) TALL AT THE SHOULDER.

Most Arabian camels are domesticated, like the Bactrians. They carry people and packages across deserts. They pull plows and haul hay. They provide people with wool for cloth, and they produce milk for them to drink.

DESERTS ARE REGIONS THAT RECEIVE LESS THAN 10 INCHES (25 CM) OF RAIN PER YEAR. DESERTS ARE ALWAYS DRY, BUT THEY ARE NOT NECESSARILY HOT. BACTRIANS LIVING IN THE GOBI DESERT OF CHINA AND MONGOLIA OFTEN SLOG THROUGH WINTER SNOW. THEIR DENSE WOOL SHIELDS THEM FROM TEMPERATURES THAT PLUNGE BELOW FREEZING. IN SUMMER THEY SHED THEIR SHAGGY COAT FOR SLEEKER HAIR THAT PROTECTS THEM FROM BLISTERING SUN.

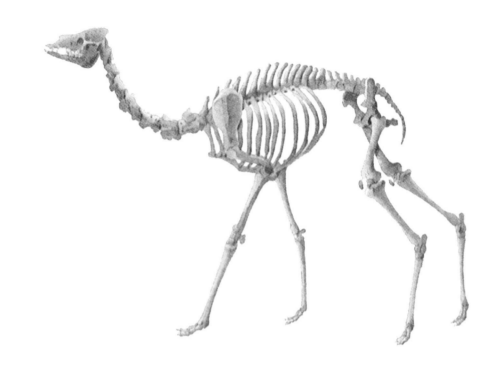

CAMELS HAVE LONG SKULLS, NECKS, AND LEGS.

Arabian camels are also raised to run in races. These special riding camels are called dromedaries. People sometimes call all Arabians dromedaries. But the term dromedary is properly used only for the swift Arabian racing breeds.

Some Arabian camels are not domesticated. But they are not wild either. They are *feral*. Feral camels wander freely. They are descended from domesticated animals that were turned loose or wandered away.

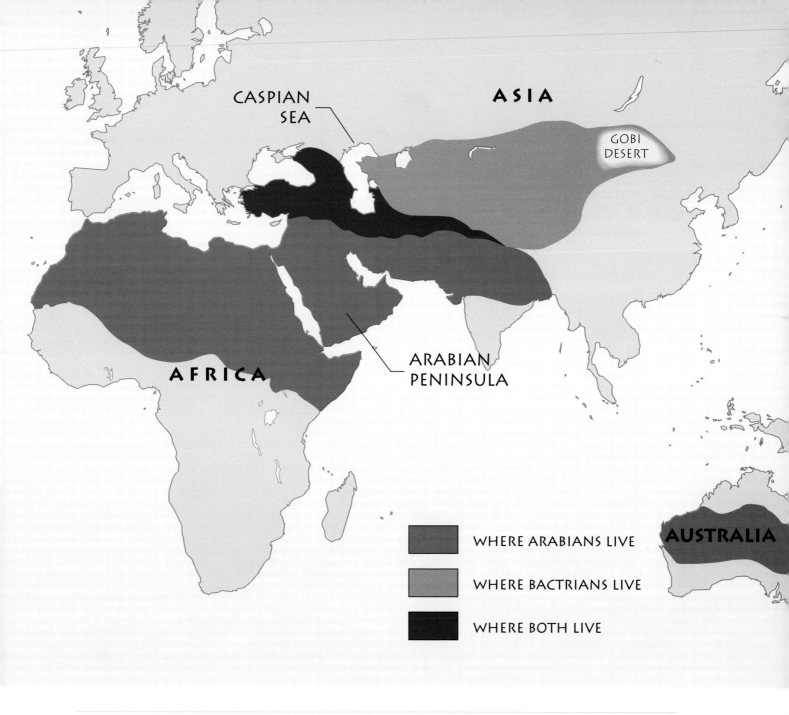

CASPIAN
SEA

ASIA

GOBI
DESERT

AFRICA

ARABIAN
PENINSULA

WHERE ARABIANS LIVE

WHERE BACTRIANS LIVE

WHERE BOTH LIVE

AUSTRALIA

CAMELS LIVE IN HOT, DRY CLIMATES IN AFRICA, ASIA, AND AUSTRALIA.

A LLAMA'S DENSE WOOL KEEPS OUT WIND AND RAIN.

Today, feral Arabian camels live in Australia's deserts. Their domesticated ancestors were shipped over from India in the mid–1800s. These camels carried mail and supplies through the desert, where horses could not survive. One camel even hauled a piano. But by the 1920s cars and trucks replaced the camels. The animals were turned loose, and their feral descendants roam Australia today.

In 1856 camels were also brought to the desert of the American southwest. They lugged supplies to settlers and to army forts from Texas to California. This experiment ended during the Civil War. No descendants of this Camel Corps remain in the American desert.

Although there are no camels in North America today, South America is home to relatives of the camel. These camel relatives are called *lamoids*. Lamoids include the domesticated llamas and alpacas and the wild guanacos and vicuñas. These animals are smaller than camels and do not have humps. They have little nimble feet for scrambling over the cold, rocky Andes mountains. Like camels, they are *herbivores*, grazing on grasses and browsing on bushes.

2
A CAMEL'S DIET

A lean, long-necked camel lowers its head to a golden patch of grass. Its upper lip wiggles over sandy plants as it snatches and snips the stems. It trims and nips a bit here and there. Always moving, a camel ambles as it eats. Unlike cattle, camels usually do not nibble plants down to their roots. Trimming plants the way camels do helps to encourage the plants to grow.

Nearby, a camel stretches its neck into a prickly bush. Thick, hairy lips search easily through the thorns. Opening its huge mouth, it snaps off a spiny stem. Sturdy teeth and a tough tongue crush the barbs and bristles. Spines and thorns are a common feature of desert plants. Thorns do not dry out easily like thin, broad leaves. Although camels can handle this spiny diet, they also eat dates and grains that their owners give them.

A CAMEL'S BOTTOM FRONT TEETH NEVER STOP GROWING. GNAWING ON TOUGH PLANTS OR ON BONES KEEPS THEM WORN DOWN.

CAMELS USE THEIR KEEN SENSE OF SMELL TO DETECT WATER HOLES AND RAINFALL.

14

Camels gather food with their strong, flexible lips. Their upper lip is split, and each side can move separately. This allows camels to grasp food as if they had fingers. Camels clip the leaves and stems with sharp teeth in the bottom jaw and tough gums in the upper jaw. Then flat teeth in the back of the jaws grind and mash the plants.

After a bit of chewing, camels swallow the wet wad of plants. Humans could not digest this fibrous material. But camels can. Camels have three stomach chambers. Tiny organisms live in the first chamber. These organisms, called *bacteria*, break down the stringy plant fibers. They turn the food into green, slimy mush.

Camels cough up balls of this partly digested food, called *cud*. They chew the cud about forty to fifty times before swallowing it. Then this chopped, chewed, soupy food enters the second and third stomach chambers. Digestion is completed there, releasing nutrients for the camel's use.

CAMELS EAT SALTY PLANTS THAT MANY DESERT ANIMALS AVOID.

Any nutrients that are not used are stored as fat. Camels do not store this fat all over their bodies, like humans. They store it in their humps. Camels draw on this fat reserve when food is scarce. As the fat is used, the humps shrink and droop. But a hearty feast will plump the hump back up.

Why do camels concentrate their fat in humps instead of spreading it out? Humps are an advantage in the broiling desert. If a camel were wrapped in a sheet of fat, it would hold in too much heat.

3
BLASTING SAND AND BLAZING SUN

Riders perched on lanky camels appear over the crest of a dune. With a slow, rolling motion, the camels wade through waves of Sahara sand. Up ahead, a wisp of wind lifts a smoky mist of dust. The sand curls and swirls up, springing at the riders. Its burning breath blows grit into their ears, eyes, and noses.

But the camels are not bothered. A screen of hair guards the entrance to their ears. Long, lush lashes and bushy brows shield their eyes. In addition, camels have a third eyelid. This lid is thin, so camels can see a bit if they keep it closed during a sandstorm. When howling winds hurl showers of dirt, camels tighten muscles in their nostrils. This narrows the openings and blocks the assault of sand.

WHEN CAMELS WALK, THEY ROCK FROM SIDE TO SIDE.

CAMELS ARE WELL ADAPTED TO
HARSH DESERTS, BUT PEOPLE
MUST COVER UP.

IN WINTER, THE BACTRIAN CAMEL'S LONG, WOOLLY COAT PROTECTS IT FROM
WINTER WEATHER IN THE GOBI DESERT.

Besides blasts of gritty dirt, camels must also cope with blistering sun. Hairy, overhanging ridges of bone shade their eyes like a visor. Long tufts of wool on their humps and heads block the blazing sun. But the hair on their bellies and sides is much shorter. This allows body heat to escape.

Sand can sometimes reach 158° F (70° C) in the summer. The tough padded feet of the camel tread over the burning dunes with no problem. People cannot bear these temperatures with open-toed sandals. They must wear woolen shoes to prevent sand from searing their feet.

In scalding heat, camels do not skitter under a shady bush or scuttle into a cool hole. Instead, they huddle together and face into the sun. Pressing against each other makes sense because their bodies are cooler than the surrounding air. And by facing toward the sun, a camel protects its wide sides from being directly heated.

A camel handles heat in another interesting way. It does not maintain a constant body temperature. Its temperature

A CAMEL'S STILTLIKE LEGS RAISE ITS BODY ABOVE THE SCORCHING SAND. IN THE SAHARA, THE AIR ONE FOOT (30 CM) ABOVE THE GROUND MAY BE COOLER THAN THE SAND BY 40 DEGREES.

CAMELS CAN RESTORE LOST WATER QUICKLY. SCIENTISTS HAVE OBSERVED THEM DRINKING AS MUCH AS 27 GALLONS (104 LITERS) IN TEN MINUTES. SUCH AN INFLUX OF WATER WOULD KILL OTHER ANIMALS. CAMELS CAN TOLERATE THIS PARTLY BECAUSE THEIR RED BLOOD CELLS CAN SWELL TO MORE THAN TWICE THEIR NORMAL SIZE WITHOUT BURSTING.

slowly climbs during the day to as much as 106° F (41° C). Only when its temperature rises above this point does the camel sweat to cool off. This saves the camel's supply of body water. In the chilly evening its temperature gradually falls to as low as 93° F (34° C). This gives its body a cool start to the next day. Because its temperature fluctuates by day and night, a camel follows the natural rhythm of the desert. This allows it to conserve water.

Camels have other ways of saving this precious fluid. They do not use much water to flush wastes from their bodies. The wastes in their urine are quite concentrated, and camel pellets are nearly dry. Under very dry conditions camels recycle the water in their breath. Instead of being exhaled, the moisture is reabsorbed inside the camel's nose. Being thrifty with water enables camels to go for long periods without drinking.

THE SAHARA MAY BE SCORCHING HOT AT MIDDAY, BUT NEAR FREEZING AT NIGHT.

A SANDSTORM KICKS UP. IN PERSISTENT STORMS, A CAMEL WILL FALL TO ITS KNEES AND STAY STILL UNTIL IT IS OVER.

Camels can lose twice as much water as people can without becoming dangerously dry, or *dehydrated.* When humans become dehydrated, most of the water is lost from their blood. The blood volume decreases, and the blood becomes thicker. The heart must strain to circulate the blood. Blood carrying heat from the center of the body does not reach the skin, where the heat can be released. Camels do not have this problem. When they become dehydrated, the water is mostly lost from inside and around the body tissues. So the blood continues to circulate normally, and heat can flow from the skin.

From their lengthy lashes to their rugged feet, camels are designed for the desert. Despite extreme conditions, they are able to survive, thrive, and raise their young.

4
BIRTH AND GROWTH

At sunset in the Sahara, the air chills and the sand glows toasty orange. A herd of Arabian camels browses casually. But one female camel leaves the herd and saunters off by herself. At daybreak, she is no longer alone. At her feet lies a curly-wooled white calf.

Thirteen months ago this mother mated with the male camel in her herd. He had chased off other males so that only he could mate with the females. Defeated males, who gather in their own herd, may challenge the lead male again next year.

The newborn calf weighs about 80 pounds (36 kilograms). It has a tiny hump and long, gangly legs. Ten minutes after it is born, it straightens its legs, trying to get up. But the skinny sticks collapse. For two hours, the calf struggles to stand. Finally, it balances for a couple of minutes before its shaky legs crumple.

A CALF'S LEGS ARE NEARLY AS LONG AS ITS MOTHER'S.

HERBIVORES DO NOT USUALLY HAVE SHARP, POINTY TEETH. BUT CAMELS DO. THESE TEARING TEETH ARE ESPECIALLY LONG IN THE MALES. THEY USE THEM TO FIGHT FOR THE RIGHT TO MATE WITH THE FEMALES.

The standing calf is about 4 feet (1.2 m) high at the shoulder. It is tall enough to reach its mother's milk. Mother's milk is its first food, as it is with all *mammals*. By its second day the calf is drinking every hour or two. But it also enjoys licking and sucking all sorts of objects.

Young calves like to nibble on plants. By two or three months they may be eating them regularly. But they still enjoy milk. Even at two or three years they will snatch a drink now and then. Herders try to *wean*, or stop calves from drinking milk, at twelve to eighteen months. This leaves more milk for the herder's family.

Sometimes camels are born when herders and their families are traveling. Since the calf will not be able to keep up, it rides on an adult camel's back. By the second day though, the calf is strong enough to follow along.

Calves and mothers keep in touch with each other by calling. The baby camel bleats like a lamb when frightened.

CAMELS GIVE BIRTH TO ONE CALF AT A TIME.

CAMELS CAN GIVE BIRTH UNTIL THEY
ARE TWENTY OR THIRTY YEARS OLD.

CURIOUS CAMEL CALVES MAY WANDER AWAY, BUT THEY COME WHEN THEIR
MOTHERS CALL.

34

If its mother comes to it without calling, the calf may not recognize her by sight. It may even run away. But when the mother calls, the calf scampers up to her.

At only four or five years a young camel is old enough to have its own calf. It is also big enough to take on a full load of work. Only with the help of camels can some people live in the desert.

5
FROM CARAVAN TO RACETRACK

In front of the Garissa Public Library in Kenya, three Arabian camels growl and groan. A frustrated librarian is trying to load the cranky camels with books, a tent, a desk, and a chair. About two hours later, the portable library is set to go. The little *caravan* is headed to the village of Marantu. No roads lead to Marantu. The only way in is by foot or by camel. There is no library in Marantu, and children have only textbooks to read.

In Marantu the librarian sets up the tent, desk, and chair, and lays out the books on the floor. The children file through. They all select books and sit under the trees with their treasures.

Camel caravans have been delivering goods for hundreds of years. Camels crossed continents before roads

A CAMEL'S LEAD ROPE IS TIED AROUND ITS JAW OR THROUGH A NOSE RING.

joined desert cities and before there were trucks, trains, and planes. In fourteenth–century Africa, camels hauled slabs of salt dug from dried–up lake beds. They carried the salt to Timbuktu, a busy caravan city where people traded it for an equal weight of gold. They also traded spices, ivory, books, and ostrich plumes.

Caravans traveled the deserts of Asia too. They linked China with countries that bordered the Mediterranean Sea. Camels carried silk and herbal medicines west. Then they returned east with jade, walnuts, glass, and perfumes.

Today camel caravans do not roam as far. But people called *nomads* still journey through the deserts of Asia and Africa. Always on the move, these nomads herd their sheep and goats from one grassy area to another. Camels carry children, water, tents, blankets, food, and kettles. They also provide milk and wool. Camel dung is used as fuel, since there are few trees in the desert. Their hides are made into buckets, tents, and sandals. Sometimes their meat is eaten.

PIRATES SAILED ON SEAGOING SHIPS. BUT SOME PIRATES RODE CAMELS, "THE SHIPS OF THE DESERT." ON SWIFT DROMEDARIES THESE DESERT PIRATES RAIDED CARAVANS OR DEMANDED GOODS IN EXCHANGE FOR PASSAGE.

ALICE SPRINGS, AUSTRALIA HOSTS AN ANNUAL CAMEL RACE.

THE ARABIC WORD FOR CAMEL, *JAMAL*, COMES FROM THE SAME ROOT WORD AS *JAMIL*, MEANING BEAUTY.

CAMELS HAVE SERVED PEOPLE FOR THOUSANDS OF YEARS. TODAY, THEY ARE USED TO TRANSPORT TOURISTS AND THEIR GEAR.

Some camels work on farms. They pull plows, turn wheels to pump water, and carry crops from the fields. Camels allow people to ride in places without roads, and some are ridden by jockeys in races. Large stadiums in Arabia and Australia hold excited crowds rooting for their favorite camel. These dromedaries are fed highly nutritious diets and put on special exercise plans. A winning camel may sell for as much as half a million dollars.

Other people who own camels give rides to tourists. In Egypt, visitors can take a camel tour around the Great Sphinx and the pyramids. In Australia, camels carry people on monthlong treks into the wilderness. Tourists can also "take a camel to lunch," on a ride to a scenic restaurant.

But to people like the Bedouin nomads of Arabia, the camel is more than an amusement. The camel is honored. Camels have made desert life possible for them and for generations of their ancestors. These people are ever thankful for all the camel has done for them. To them the camel is *Ata Allah*–"God's gift."

bacteria: Organisms that are too small to be seen without a microscope. Bacteria in a camel's stomach break down fibrous plant material.

caravan: A group of people and animals journeying together across a desert.

cud: Partially digested food that an animal brings up from its stomach and chews again.

dehydrated: Without a normal amount of water or moisture.

domestic: An animal that is taken care of by people.

feral: A free roaming animal that was formerly domesticated or that is descended from domesticated animals.

herbivore: An animal that feeds chiefly on plants.

lamoids: Animals in the camel family, which include South American wild guanacos and vicuñas and domesticated llamas and alpacas.

mammal: A warm–blooded animal with a backbone that has fur or hair, gives birth to live young, and makes milk to feed its young.

nomads: People who do not live in one set place. They move about following the food and water supply.

species: A particular type of living thing.

wean: To gradually withhold mother's milk from a young animal.

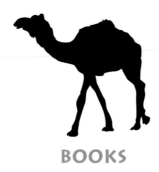

BOOKS

Arnold, Caroline. *Camel.* New York: Morrow Junior Books, 1992.

Bailey, Donna. *Camels.* Austin, TX: Steck–Vaughn Company, 1991.

Cloudsley–Thompson, John. *Camels.* Milwaukee, WI: Raintree Children's Books, 1980.

Dawson, Susie. *Camels.* Danbury, CT: Grolier Educational, 1999.

Green, Carl R. *The Camel.* Mankato, MN: Crestwood House, 1988.

Kenworthy, Leonard S. *Camels and Their Cousins.* New York: Harvey House, 1975.

Markert, Jenny. *Camels.* Chanhassen, MN: The Child's World, Inc., 1991.

Raskin, Lawrie with Deborah Pearson. *52 Days by Camel: My Sahara Adventure.* New York: Annick Press, 1998.

Wexo, John Bonnett. *The Camel Family.* Poway, CA: Wildlife Education, Ltd., 2001.

MAGAZINES

Hankom, Luann. "Journey on the Silk Road." *Appleseeds,* October 2002: 12–15.

Hare, John. "Surviving the Sahara." *National Geographic,* December 2002: 54–77.

Jordan, Ann. "The Amazing Camel: Ship of the Desert." *Appleseeds,* April 2002: 20–21.

Schneider, Linda. "Camels." *Ranger Rick,* January 2001: 22–23.

WEB SITES

The A–Z of Camels

www.arab.net/camels/

Africa: Dromedary Camel

www.oaklandzoo.org/atoz/azcamel.html

Camels . . . The Ships of the Desert

www.ecssr.ac.ae/Land/camels.html

Dromedary and Bactrian Camel Information

www.all–animals.com/bcamels.html

How the Camel Got His Hump

www.boop.org/jan/justso/camel.htm

Planet Camel

www.planet-pets.com/plntcaml.htm

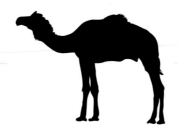

ABOUT THE AUTHOR

Judith Jango-Cohen's intimate knowledge of nature comes from years of observing and photographing in swamps, canyons, caves, and glaciers. Her twenty-eight children's books reflect these experiences. They have been listed in Best Books for Children, recommended by the National Science Teacher's Association, and chosen for the Children's Literature Choice List. You can find photos from the many trips she has taken with her family at www.agpix.com/cohen.

Page numbers for illustrations are in **boldface.**